SIRENS

SIRENS
TONI OSWALD

GESTURE PRESS
DENVER, CO

Copyright © Toni Oswald, 2020
Cover art © Kelsey Cruz-Martin
Interior art © Caitlin Alesandra
Author photo © Max Davies

Interior and cover design by Heather Goodrich and HR Hegnauer

Gesture Press
Denver, CO
gesturepressandjournal.com

ISBN: 978-0-578-77394-0
Cataloging-in-publication data is available from the Library of Congress.

First Edition | First Printing
Printed in the United States of America

For Nuit

PART ONE

Sold a hole to a disaster
Nail the strong winds tied to a door
Know the crimes that stick in thru
Unfastened belts on your heart
And I've never been very smart
But I connect you with your shadow

—Niandra LaDes

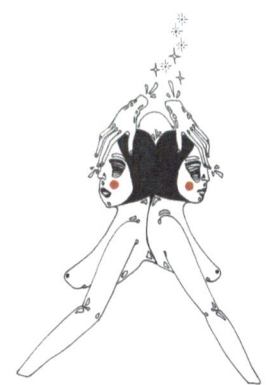

PROLOGUE

There was Dream in the Land of Mirrors

We are in a dream.
We run to the mirror.
We look into the mirror.

A woman runs to the window,
Her hand a prayer on the glass of night,
"I know you are! I know WHO you are!"

But there is no one there.

Sometimes things will sound backward,
                like walking through a building into a lake

You might have encountered strange things before,
      but these things are much stranger.

Imagine a pie cut into eight pieces,

                            each piece a different kind of blue.

Behold
I show you a mystery
falling through space

Before wings
back in a dream
before the first life
you fell through the stars
hearing laughter on the way down

It began as a lark
bursting of floodgates—
faint and quivering
via dolorosa

Where the bones guide us
we go now
from jaggedness
jaw breaks
into a thousand blue wings

Things are much stranger than we had imagined.

Her was born part bird

formed in a blue egg
a feathered one with wings—hatched

a beak
and girl parts too.

Her would fit in the palm of a child's hand and sing a song of smiles—innocence (which connects to spirit) was lifted up as moonlight.

Heaven screams the baby driver out
where bold cocks dress up as little girls
        this is where we make the feminine
                Jasmine binds the seal

Friction creates the fountain
    find your baby
    calling you in
you are the lie that must be told

Enter here
shake out the fear
you have fallen into this world
the path is snake.

Her landed into a place where only bones could guide her,
inside the lip of the female a fledgling resounds—

(say it out loud with me)

eeeeeee

        aaaaay

                eeeeye

                        ahhhhh

                                ohhhhh

                                        oooooo

                                              uhhhhh

                                        eeeeee

                                aaaaay

                          eeeeye

                    ahhhhh

              ohhhhh

        oooooo

uhhhhh

Baby birds are of two types:

The first is Atricial, born without feathers, eyes closed, relying in extensor on their parents for warmth and food. Fragile, fragile, they must be fed every 15-20 minutes, from sunset to sunrise.

The second Precocial break open as soft down chicks, soon able to follow their parents around, not needing their help at all. They follow their mother around imprinting her warmth and protection.

Her was a hybrid:

she had feathers and eyes to see, but needed her parents completely.

100 million years ago birds came and flew.

Her also came to fly.

In the beginning she played with geometry and light

tiny hands became a mirror of the sun, casting shadow to shape the day.

Her light is something other
heterodox ()
           a luminous O

    but we are light laid out in darkness
                            we spin to turn

women turn to spin
                to spin through

                                  what is only this lifetime
So many
            in one
                    spinning.

The dervish spins

        to touch

                the thread of God.

  We spin the web

        casting spell

                spin the loom

all is spinning

         being is spun

    spun into being.

spin the loom

      spin to turn

         this woman's work,

This is

        Her.

Humans watched birds fly and wondered.

Running and jumping, they flapped their arms. In trees they perched, ready to rise, "Carry us towards heaven," they cried as they leapt, but their bones were dense and gravity broke them.

Smitten by air *Her* also dreamed of flying: weight lift drag thrust.

Certain little girls and little boys have flown.

Like honeycomb they have hollow bones: airy and strong/weight lift drag thrust.

Early on there was a purpose.

The humans did not think it okay for *Her* to be a bird and so they clipped her wings.

Her now a she without wings sat bleeding in a bathtub; in some versions of the story the paramedics arrived in time, and in others, did not.

Your hands just turned blue:

Ever since she could remember, rooms were all she had

                                                     What was surrounding *Her*

        She who is

            in here

                            She understands certain things (like what it means to fly)

            illusions are hardest (what is this world?)
                  She imagined *Her*
                          in me

                                                in us

                ghosts from hand to mouth.

Hoo Hoo

bells   beak   spirit
façade breaks who?

greed   eats   soul

whose hollow man are you?

Here goes another us.

But am I saying there is a way out
in an instant to see the total movement of life as yourself?

Time is all cut up
I saw you in a dream
We were five.

                                                I realize you have been fooled—
                                                             So have I.

WE are ALL writing this.

We are lost.
We are trying to find our way back.

Let there be light:
Let it enter our darkness

And drown in the mystery of the world.

A crow flew into the dream you are having right now:

While picking strawberries,
we arrive on the sorcerer's shore.
Still looking for our lost selves,
we hear grieving
                waves crashing

In vain, we attempt to fill the hole that will not be filled

        Even so, broken birds become sirens of sorrow.
        Sail carefully—their song is everywhere.

Our eyes not our own,
we wear someone else's glasses
Our sight disturbed by what we see.

Do you understand what is happening?

A Riddle

Get out your special magnifying glass:

I am part of what you used to be and you are part of what I used to be

dirt
a stem a branch a trunk a root a seed
an apple
a bear
a crane
a piece of tape
a rugged terrain somewhere in Colorado
possible human
an animal
a bird   a her   a him   a we

(Think on this for two minutes)

it's *H*appening

on *E*arth

Remember

PART TWO

We have passed the great trauma
These wounds disclose our loss
—Mina Loy

There is a fever.
The sound of whispering.
              Spspspspspspspspspspspspspspspspspspspsps

The head has gone inward, a mad horse. It rides any thought it finds.
              Spspspspspspspspspspspspspspspspspspspsps

Horse bit clenched—unflinching darkness.
Down here in the deep it is dark and cool; above ground it burns.
              Spspspspspspspspspspspspspspspspspspspspsps

I look for our dreams: They fell into a bottomless pit.

Womb constricts, We /0\ am /0\ barren; tumors make knots unwindable.

Knocking, these are our dreams; lost children painting stories in blue.
HOOOOOOOOOTTTTTT

I cannot bear this heat anymore. Am I exploding?
Below this night everything vibes chimerical, cimmerian.

A cavern of wonder beneath the fire.
I've become used to this heat, this fire, this loss, everything burned up—
this siren's song.

Icarus's unnamed daughter falling
Spspspspspspspspspspspspspspspspspspspsps

I burn up and then I drown
again and again, the cycle continues.

My wings are charred broken charcoal limbs.
        the heat is sexual and has gone off like a mad bitch. *Her*

I am burned up with this desire locked in my hotness, a box.
I made it myself and put these things in it: A nightgown from childhood, a bag of pills
my old 45 records
that painting of the monkey
and some spit.

I placed them all in a box and set it ablaze.
I'm not me anymore.
I am only a bird you knew:
                                  The fire, the fire, fire fire THE FIRE.

The fever has taken me, I see the angels,
that old black tooth as well—
there is chalk, whiteness, and the dark lady.
Hopscotching on my driveway—I jump.
Oh little deer, how I've missed you.

Where are the blues?

        I   can   not
I cannot see
that blackness   (the sea in me)
the blue darkling   *we shadow*

the black black black   the blue blue blue
                burning pie blues

4 cups flour, 1tsp salt, bake at 350, bake at 400, bake at 450
    My head hurts *she puts her head in the oven just like this*
                              Spspspspspspspspspspspspspspspspspspsps

Early that morning she stood on the sidewalk waiting for her man Coco.

The glamour of fatality: red lips, white powder, raccoon eyes, black mink coat to score. She stood on West 47th her only weapon held in her hand: a box of imagination.

Later, she lay in bed among scarves with a dreariness she had failed to predict, "Oh Virginia," she said to herself. "I understand it is hell sometimes."

Vapors from Her smoke float and caress as she slips inside the dazzling air. She drives up and over burned out boys dismembered. Does anyone realize we are at war and what that means? The Lieutenant, man-sized now, rises, "Something is rotten, no doubt we've gone wrong."

   a husk
   not a piece
   a vein bent low
   a single note—NO
   nothing stands alone

"Look out sailor, this siren's had enough."

There is no way we've had enough: stepping into broken mirrors, weight of arms, a life of private remembering. Will you always go there?

Her: How far out did we actually go?

   In space a fall looks like a blur.

Her was working for a large fish looking man who hired girls to work as high-class whores among other things. *Her* drove him around, did 'things" for him. He hit her hard when *Her* talked back. *Her* knew then how to survive.

Looking through the rearview mirror at him, "I was just trying to look pretty for you," *Her* said, as she reapplied scarlet lipstick, then white powder where he smacked *Her* in the face.

Her drove the car through the city while he lounged in back.

He was with another girl who also worked for him. He got his cock out, which was hard and smooth; he rubbed it against the girl's pussy.

The girl got so turned on—so horny rubbing her panties on his rod. Even though she hated his bulging eyes, his sweaty face, his bulbous lips—everything about him. The froggy way he moved sucked everything in sight.

The girl pulled aside her panties; it was inside then and he was so fell and crude, but she could not control the way it made her feel alive (then dead).

The girl begged him for it.

And in the end, there was only a white stain across black leather—humans have thrown so much beauty away.

Her knew that seeing this she would never be free of the siren's song. *Her* observed herself in the glass reflection of the window; her lips slightly parted, on the verge of a scream, her eyes blue waves filled with crashing boats.

You recognize *Her* as someone other than who she am.

    Her is a watcher
    Her is a good nothing
    Her is a good nowhere

    the World asks *Her* to be a lie
    to Be an artful manipulator
    to Make herself special

    This is not truth
    but the world is hung up on lies
    forgetting Who is Hoo

    others coming through *Her*
    where does she end and we begin?

She plays the part, the great actress
it gives *Her* a certain power over we the world

Her needs the power for she has lost her wings

    Buried under the lies
    buried
    but is she really gone?

In some parts of reality, girls are sold and their organs are harvested for rich people in the West who have lost something.

Under Geranium wallpaper *Her* will give you a bath, a suck, a fuck, and get only some of the money from the men running the show.

The Magdalene was a priestess, you stupid fucks.

But sex is wicked, and women are second class citizens.

This equals prostitution, children sold and raped, economic slavery, rich men coming into poor (be)little(d) girls.

A river of death made from semen, blood, and lies.

I think the Magdalene fucked Christ beatifically.

like a heartbeat,
like a step,
like a stairway to Heaven.

(Somewhere down below)

In *Her* nightmares she witnesses a carnival:

Every ride made of weapons: "Step right up!" shouts the barker dressed in fatigues. "Ride the Browning M2 .50 caliber Machine gun for only a nickel."

Calliope churns the smoke-filled air. Children vomit exiting the fun house.

Next stop, the carousel of bombs—feel the power of empire between your thighs—

Don't forget the Tanks 'R Us finale, where for just a quarter, you can trample your enemies, no questions asked.

A merry-go-round of knives spinning, war machine of death turning.

"Hear the laughter?" *(Smell the tears)*

It's a dark game the world is playing at. *(Run for your life)*

Step onto this road made of salt.
Down on your knees bend over and taste its sorrow.
Ahead are thousands of women, all made of tears.

They are all me. They are all you. They are all us.

Look at the body of a *Her:*

The sharp angular bones where the wings once attached.
Do you see the door the wounds make?

Let us enter to find what has been lost.
                    Is anything ever found?

Her body does resemble a universe. Look closer. An atmosphere unto itself: air, fire, water, earth.

Ancient hieroglyphs descend from head to foot—a map of what has been will be. Scars as watermarks, remnants of various emotions reaching through space time tomb. Fear turns into a strange beauty when the eye focuses and the mind forgets. Breath, heart pumping, a spleen is overworked; anemia sets in to the abandoned womb. The kidneys cry and piss all over everything. *Her* skin yellows, the whites of her eyes rolling rancid; she is a monster.

It took thirteen days for the woman to die. She was gang raped and beaten by a busload of men, including the bus driver. They even beat her male friend traveling with her.

Her broke stairs that descended into bones that look like teeth.

On the day they found her, she lay crying on a stone floor, where she was attempting to cool her back; she was covered in blisters from shoulder blades to buttocks. A few days before, her owners poured hot oil on her for working too slowly. She was eleven years old.

There is a falcon soaring, there above the skin sky, where lightening lurks. An electrical canyon painted red/beautiful murals of death where seeds fall through the cracks.

Her is breaking down—crying like a baby, a fire, a blaze of bats out from under a bridge.

Grieving mothers gather in the streets and cry out, "Why do you kill our children?"

Inch by inch of *Her* carries the truth in her song, but her lips have been sewn shut with strings of radiation, and now the whole world is at stake.

She was six when they tied her to a bush—three women held her down while one sat on her chest and covered her mouth. A woman with empty eyes came forward with a sharp blade, grabbed her clitoris and CUT.

Move forward to the brain. Our circuits are looped to repeat doom.

Shit out the poison. Fertilize the pink calcite *Her* put all of her dying dreams into. Bury those crystals behind the lake of blue smoke and let mushrooms grow from their shit to feed the world.

Spray-painted on an alley in red:

We know who you bastards are, and we will reclaim the parts that make the whole.

I am cutting all of the shes free—

                                                                        Cut-cut slice

    Who am I?
           You do not need to know.

                                                     Think of me as a pair of scissors.

Cut-cut slice   cut-cut slice

PART THREE

Your magic will be better
than their magic.

–Jack Spicer

STITCH: one complete movement of a threaded needle through a fabric or material such as to leave behind a single loop or portion of thread, as in sewing, embroidery, *or the surgical closing of wounds.*

The *Stitch* may be invisible but it is there nonetheless.

Do you remember your birth and falling into this?
Will you ever let go of that mourning?

There must be a will,
To rescue oneself.

Women in blue robes stand at the edge of the chasm singing a song:

> *We remember black soil brimming with beetles.*
> *We remember rivers overflowing with salmon.*
> *We remember cool mist on mountains and the wisdom of plants.*
> *We remember the song of sunrise, and the whisper of dusk.*
> *Do you remember Us and Our Song?*

Orange flowers fly from their hands becoming ghosts ships set sail for death has come to the hubris of man.

That evening *Her* grew enormous, stretching spine, hair as sail, jagged teeth cutting her lips, a maniac filled mud, blood and oil.

In *Her* mind there was only the sound of a loud rage—blue black teeth hissing whiskey and rot. Time hid behind Uranus (not Jupiter).

the ghost the ghost the ghost the ghost the ghost the ghost the ghost the ghost
The train was moving fast as we stood on the edge of the open rail car.

"Where do you end and I begin?" I asked.

"It's all mixed up," she yelled over the roar, squinting through the gleam.

"I wish," I whispered, "I could say I don't care what happens next."

"But you do and I won't live as her again," she said coolly, her eyes a flock of geese crossing the sky above us.
the ghost the ghost the ghost the ghost the ghost the ghost the ghost the ghost

"You've always been here," I said grasping her arm, afraid she might jump   /\

"But I'm so tired of dirty dishes, so tired of cooking the same thing week after week, dusting and sweeping and weeping."

I let go of her arm and did what had to be done—
I threw a certain Sylvia off the train. *we shadow*

                                                         I pushed her off. Had to.

She was smiling right before she hit the field of poppies.
Her braids rose like horns spiraling. *Spspspspspspspspspspsps*

Angel birds swooped down and lifted her up.
       the ghost the ghost the ghost the ghost the ghost the ghost the ghost the ghost

   angel birds lifted her up   *their song a black tear lip*
   lifted Her   *blood oil greased the edges surrounding death*
   Up   *shapeshifting*
   lifted her uP   *polished gold became her crown*   and *we shadow*

     the ghost the ghost the ghost the ghost the ghost the ghost the ghost the ghost
                                  carried *Her* away

Lightning cracked platinum heat
rumble of thunder rolled across her back, deluged by rain

She went blind and cried for the already extinct, the dying, the nameless,
all the stories never told
from her navel emerged
lizard with two diamond eyes slouching towards the lie of the world:

"You will pay in more ways than you can possibly imagine," it hissed as the sky
turned gray and swallowed the fire in her spine.

Her howled wet with gleam
tears fell and formed a ship she stepped into
taken up by the clouds
upwards the rain in reverse:
uP uP uP

Into the night—*her*.

The ship crashes into a field, scattering salt Beneath an ice sky flurries of snow shape shift into bees made of mirrors buzzing toward *Her*.

Rot rises from the chasm:

        a black pot where we mix:

        1 part madness
        1 part genius
        1 teaspoon of sulfur
        1 teaspoon of blood

        Stir to make a *Her*

We smell female:

Her slithers closer, pressing her body against the we—
    Salt thickens her tongue, becoming numb *Her* is nothing but a thought.

No sight. No sound.
the ghosts   the ghosts   the ghosts

We are inside the eye
of the other

        Skin parts
           open:
           there is pelage too.

We float and bend:

"*Drop down, drop down!*" we shout.

Her lay by the heels, pushing through mud into earth. *Her* wings become roots spiraling downward into the center

We feel the scission between bone and wing: a clean break as we sail away singing.

A thousand spirits are flying out of the dream of the world.

All of this is being said much later.
        Spoke to the ways we come into the outside of time.

Her emerges from the mud
wings await
woven of grass and spit of bees
stitched upon the night
eagle feathers dipped in gold
spanning out, her shadow vast
diaphanous effluvium
light delivered from darkness

(police sirens in the distance)

Her flies up—there is only the sound of wings flapping
                                      and the feeling of *Her* smiling

Below she watches the world's lies
fall like dominoes;

they fall, fall

and fall.

Landing on the edge of a lake

She dips her toes in red ink
She takes her body down into the
red ink
everywhere: spilled across the land, written on air, blue-ing with water
    and *Her* in it
    up to her neck
    she lets herself fall back
    becoming red ink *made of star we shadow*

Where thousands of sparrows fly out, she moves through
wings tipped red red ink
they rise and fly from out of the crack in the sky *wake up*
they fly out, they fly out out
out of her mind, they fly *we shadow*
    and there is no madness but
    absolute clarity as *Her*
    steps out of the pool
    her body she rolls across the road, writing words in red—wake up.

She cradles us while
speaking in tongues

We come through the door of perception while fucking
folded and golden.

See us now in the quilt of
rusted sanity, where a cross-stitch
looms so fair; it is here in these
dreams, we pluck back the false reeds
releasing all else from the snare.

Go ahead. Laugh at the void. She did. It was hilarious.

We cup *Her* bowl with bantam hands and immerse it into the milk laid like lake before *Her*.

We tilt the earth back and drink from it; her breast our life, our broken veins becoming blue again.

We step into *her* milk, swim to the center of it.

We are the children: *her* shadows.

There is no fear.

Not anymore.

Formerly a whisper

Her has risen.

When the poison breaks there is transfigured light.
We have found out that what was lost could not be lost.

The ocean has swallowed hysteria; fear was left somewhere biting and lightless, its knives and fists sewn into seven wheels that spin beneath the red house I saw last night in your dream. A place where a woman told me, "Hold your gaze to that corner and your body will disappear, then take up the thread."

Embroidering a dress with stories, truth arrives in the eye of the needle as we prick the stitch. We watch *Her* glide across the dress remembering the feminine and the fist, how it got to this: earth lubricated by oil for thousands of years— Ha-Ha they laughed and cheered, but now the pussy's dried up and won't be fucked. Wipe your tears and stop waiting for someone else to do your work. Stitch a snake for the conquerors, then let them know it's headed straight for their assholes—a place where all pleas went ignored.

Now we wander, human sorrow shaking, bending until breaking, trembling before the mountain of *precious*—all of our *stuff*. The animals and plants shake their heads, "Stupid Fuckers," I bet they're thinking, just like Anne said. And now there's nowhere to go, unless you believe billionaires who dream of Mars. Are you as tired of those fuckers as I am?

The black cycle turns, the black cycle circling all. *Her* draws the sword, spins the loom. Watch *Her* hands unravel, fingertip spools of thread. Stitch-stitch-stitch—only the finest needlework will save us from this mess. Horsewomen rise from a hole in the dress as the hem announces a she at your feet. Kiss kiss—there are only *her* lips as the helmet of Nuit surrounds you. Along the sash we lay heads to oblivion and settle the stars

                        that

                                drop

                                          from

                                                    your

                                                                   waist.

re-entering the World
contact can be strange

We study ourselves to forget ourselves: (a paradox)
then we become one with ten thousand things: (we touch the glass and we become all glass)

Notice how we play with reality: (born a bird, become a girl, born a boy, become a siren)

So much of what we've been taught is so not true

Belief is the key - to unstitching

There is no hiding in memories.
                                              Sorrow is a box.

                                                                    Let go of everything you think you know.

Her is speaking:

                    You have everything you need
                    If you only knew

                    If *we* only knew.

(Ancest(*her*))

A ghost
stands center circle
white mole guards four directions
a black moon and an earth moon take to corners *(like the woman said)*
where *we* have no map
where no one knows this ghost

This ancestor holds a black rose
symbolic ghost of blood
a resurrection
of crimson cloth

Yolk to yolk
like a wheel
this circle has spoke of *her*

When it dries cast cakes
white flour mixes with gauze
sand it—a rain of silver powder
ghosts there sirens
memory dust
holds her whisper back
we cannot imagine the sound

Spspspspspspspspspspspspspspsps

Yolk to yolk
like a wheel
this circle has spoken   *spspspspspspspspspspspspspspspspspsps*
stretched taught it
holds the path in place

Twelve circles
ten lead to another world
epic journey of DNA swims our veins

When we leave this world, we will have no eyes.

There are times I cry every time I see a tree. There are so many questions, that is the only answer.

Let's be friends even when there is no us. Let's carry it all through the dust and the sand and the smoke and the mud and all of those beautiful notes of music.

Song of the Sirens

We have come so far
      won't you see your shadow is painted on all you adore.

Please believe whatever you can if it gets you to Her
or rather drown

sunblazed
or
moonstruck

                it makes no difference
                one is one
                one is another
                it is all one thing in the end.

Love in every language.

EPILOGUE

Trust is such a difficult verb
But you are the dreamer dreaming.

ACKNOWLEDGMENTS

I'd like to thank all those who read this book in manuscript at various stages and offered wise counsel. CA Conrad, Jade Lascelles, Georgia Van Gunten, Carla Campbell, Dan Hoy, Maggie Wells, and Sarah Elizabeth Schantz.

Thanks to Ambrose Bye and Anne Waldman for including Prelude on Harry's House Vol. 3 & to Amanda Ngoho Reavy for playing cello on the track.

A huge shout out to my writing community, inside and outside of (W)rites of Passage, and roundabout Colorado's Front Range: Sarah Elizabeth Schantz, Jade Lascelles (biggest hugs + band and dance party forever = your friendship means the world to me), Heather Goodrich, Erin Jendras, HR Hegnauer, Selah Saterstrom, Laird Hunt, Eleni Sikelianos, CA Conrad (pinky-hugs), Julie Patton, Harris Armstrong, Ella Longpre, Nicolas Weseley, Madeline Seltzer, Swanee Astrid, Mairead Case, Jona Fine, Carla Campbell, Amanda Cosler, Reed Bye, Junior Burke, Richard Froude, No Land, Sherri Pauli, Rod Brakes (Yeah, I've extended the Front Range all the way to Bath, England), Naropa University's Jack Kerouac School & Summer Writing Program, and of course, Mama Poetry herself—Ms. Anne Waldman. Thank you all for your continued support and inspiration on this journey called writing.

Thank you to Heather Goodrich at Gesture Press for believing in this project and for all of the work you've done to make it the best and most beautiful book possible. Eternal respect for your vision of writing and publishing.

Thank you to Caitlin Alesandra for the beauty you are on the page, and in life. Your illustrations are more than I could ever have hoped for. Your magic is OG sister. LOVE.

Thank you to John Frusciante for the use of the Niandra LaDes lyric from his album *Niandra LaDes & Usually Just a T-Shirt*.

Thank you to Kelsey Cruz-Martin. You made my dream cover come to life! I am so honored to call you a friend and a collaborator. Let's get this art party started and take it across the world.

Thanks to Jonas Leuenberger for photographing the *Sirens* films & to Adelia Leuenberger for being the sweetest and most magical young bird girl.

A huge thank you to HR Hegnauer for her guiding light in the design of this book. Your book mojo is real magic, and we could not have made it to the finish line without your help.

HIHIHI to The Wilds: Lady Datura, Delia Ophelia, Henry Z. Flux, Elias "Solartooth" Boone & Strawberry Fontaine Forever.

Beyond thanks to the wonderful poets and writers who blurbed this book, and that I'm lucky enough to call my friends: CA Conrad, HR Hegnauer, Selah Saterstrom, Thurston Moore, and Sarah Elizabeth Schantz. Y'all help me navigate this beautiful, yet sorrowful world. Biggest brightest love to you all and utmost respect.

Deepest thanks to my mom and dad for always supporting my dreams. I love you both so much.

A special thanks to my dearest friend, Sarah Elizabeth Schantz. Words cannot explain how much I love you and thank you from the bluest blue of my heart for your friendship, support, and instruction. I couldn't have done it without you. Let's be friends even when there is no us!

And, always my Max. You make me a better woman, a better writer, a better human. Loving you is the easiest and best thing I've ever done. Thank you for all you are.

And lastly, thanks to the Sirens who call on us to dive for the deepest pearls in the Great Big Blue.

TONI OSWALD

is a writer, musician, & visual artist who lives in Boulder, Colorado. Her work has been shown and performed across the United States and Europe. She is currently working on a novel about a 14-year-old girl clown set in the 1950s. You can find her musical alter ego, The Diary of Ic Explura, on Bandcamp.

Find more of Toni's work and performances:
tonioswald.blogspot.com
@toniroxanneoswald on Instagram